Dowsing the Crop Circles

NEW INSIGHTS INTO THE GREATEST OF MODERN MYSTERIES

Edited and Introduced by John Michell

GOTHIC IMAGE PUBLICATIONS

The articles in this publication first appeared in Issues 3 and 4 of THE CEREALOGIST, the journal for crop circle studies.
THE CEREALOGIST is published three times a year; subscriptions are available from *20 Paul Street, Frome, Somerset BA11 1DX, England* UK £7.50, overseas £9.00 or $18.00 (airmail).

First published in book form in 1991 by
GOTHIC IMAGE PUBLICATIONS
7, High Street, Glastonbury, Somerset BA6 9DP
Reprinted 1992

Aerial photographs and swirl diagrams by Roland Pargeter. Crop formation silhouettes computer-generated by Richard Elen from his own work and from drawings by Richard Fraser. Individual illustrations are not to the same scale.

Designed and set in 11/12 pt. New Baskerville by Richard Elen at Creative Technology Associates, Somerton, Somerset. Printed by Castle Cary Press, Somerset.

British Library Cataloguing in Publication Data

Dowsing the crop circles: new insights into the greatest of modern mysteries
I. Michell, John.
001.94
ISBN 0 906362-17-2

CONTENTS

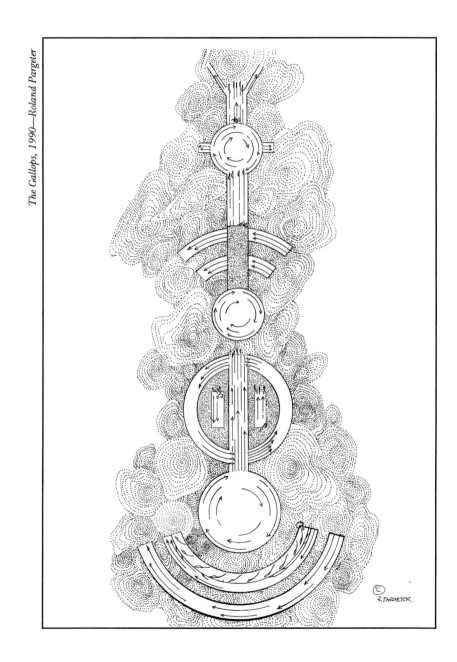

The Gallops, 1990—Roland Pargeter

Introduction
by John Michell

Richard Fraser

The antiquity of earth divination

DIVINATION THROUGH the powers of the earth is among the earliest of human arts. The first nomadic tribes lived entirely through their relationship to the earth spirit which guided their migrations, and when nomadism gave way to settlement and agriculture, priestly diviners located the proper sites for shrines and temples at centres of terrestrial energy. Earth oracles and places of resort for healing and fertility were discovered by the same references.

The spiritual energies of the earth (known to Chinese geomancers as *ch'i*, to the early Christians as the Holy Spirit and to mystical scholars by the number 1080) are everywhere conditioned in their flow by the features of the local landscape, its mountains, woods, rivers and valleys. They can also be affected by human activities, and the ancient science of priestcraft was largely concerned with detecting and manipulating the sacred energies of earth. The traditional eastern technique for founding a temple included the finding by divination of the 'dragon's head' (the dragon or earth serpent being a universal symbol of the earth spirit) and driving a stake through it, thus fixing and augmenting its energies on the appropriate site for the temple's inner sanctum.

Plutarch, who was a priest at Delphi in the first century A.D., refers in *The Decline of Oracles* to the streams of earth energy which activated oracles and places of invocation. They are, he said, influenced by the sun and the heavenly bodies. The ancient priestly science was thus concerned equally with astronomy and with divination through the earth. In secular western cultures this science has long been redundant and virtually forgotten.

In recent years, however, the need to re-establish an ecologically and spiritually balanced code of conduct between humanity and earth has drawn attention to the ancient science, now generally referred to as geomancy. Pioneer researchers in this field, including astro-archaeologists, ley hunters, geologists and dowsers, have concentrated largely upon stone circles and other prehistoric ritual sites. Almost the entire present generation of crop circle dowsers began or developed their practice thorough dowsing at megalithic monuments.

Modern dowsing and earth energies

The use of the divining rod or pendulum for locating water or mineral veins is traditional and old-established throughout the world, but in western Europe the dowsing of subtle energies at ancient sanctuaries and crop circles seems new and unfamiliar. Legends of apparitions, magical rings and healing powers linger around megalithic sites, but materialistic archaeology has had no interest in such things, and it was not until the 1930s that certain dowsers began to be aware of anomalous energy patterns at ancient monuments.

In 1935 two French archaeologists, Merle and Diot, published their findings, obtained through dowsing, that "every megalithic monument, without exception, was sited in relation to underground streams, which abut them or cross beneath them or surround them". Reginald Smith of the British Museum reported similarly in papers to the British Society of

Dowsers, and in 1969 appeared the most influential book on archaeological dowsing, Guy Underwood's *Patterns of the Past*. Drawing his examples mostly from the Wessex area (like Terence Meaden and other notables of our time he lived in Bradford-on-Avon), Underwood claimed that every old monument and building had been designed in relation to the patterns of terrestrial energy at their sites. These patterns could be discovered by dowsing.

Also influential were the books of T.C. Lethbridge, a respected archaeologist who made use of the diviner's pendulum for discovering and dating antiquities. This led him deep into the world of mysticism, and he came to perceive that stone circles had been charged by ancient priests with magical powers which still lingered. At the Merry Maidens circle in Cornwall, he and his wife were shocked by a discharge of energy, and Lethbridge formed the idea that stone circles were beacon stations for space travellers. His views were widely disseminated by the polymathic Colin Wilson.

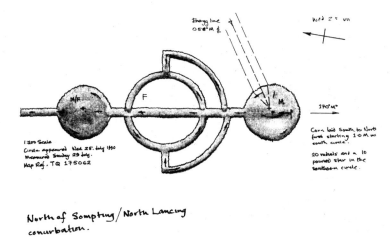

Surveyed and dowsed by David and Ba Russell, this striking 1990 pictogram appeared near Lancing, Sussex.

Enthusiasms, doubts and queries

Like novice ley hunters who begin (after exposure to Watkins's *Old Straight Track*) by drawing lines between three points all over maps, the first generation of 'energy dowsers' were unrestrained in their claims and enthusiasm. Tom Graves's *Needles of Stone* opened minds to the idea of healing the earth through her acupuncture points, following the presumed practice of the megalith builders. This perception as assimilated in various forms into New Age thinking.

Through the 1980s, British dowsers were joined by groups of American enthusiasts, armed with pendulums and diving rods, at stone circles all over the British Isles. A peak was reached at the Harmonic Convergence event of 1987, when bands of New Age missionaries from America took over and ritualised at megalithic 'power spots', sometimes (as at Callanish) to the resentment of native celebrants!

About twelve years ago, Paul Devereux began the Dragon Project, a long-term investigation of the mysterious energies, hinted at in folklore, which dowsers and others claimed to detect at megalithic sites. Experts on geo-magnetism and other scientific subjects were involved, together with dowsers and 'channelers'. In the course of time, however, the dowsers proved so inconsistent that Paul lost interest in them, though recognising that some of them (particularly such wise and unassuming veterans as Bill Lewis of Wales) were genuinely sensitive to the earth's subtle energies. As editor of *The Ley Hunter* journal, he was first puzzled and then distressed by the flood of articles he received on archaeological dowsing, many of them consisting of personal impression and fantasies with no objective relevance to his subject.

Moreover, the energy dowsers had the impudence to hijack the Watkinsian term, 'ley' (a straight alignment of ancient sites), adapt it to 'leyline' and use it as their name for the undulating currents of earth energy which they follow with their dowsing rods.

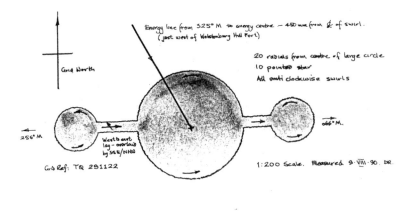

Energy line from 525° M to energy centre - 450 mm from ⅊ of swirl.
(just west of Wolstonbury Hill Fort)

20 radials from centre of large circle
10 pointed star
All anti clockwise swirls

Grid North

256° M

West b east
log - overlaid
by SSE/NNW

Grid Ref: TQ 291122

066° M.

1:200 Scale. Measured 9·VIII·90. DR.

This is now disturbed by the new dual carriageway

Working with dowsers at ancient sites, Devereux observed that their reported findings were often widely different. This, he was surprised to find, did not seem to worry them at all. They enjoyed the excitement of following their rod or pendulum, but in general they seemed unconcerned about whether or not other dowsers reported the same pattern of 'leylines', forms of energy or historical impressions as they themselves. If these people can not agree among themselves or produce any coherent information, concluded Devereux, their activities are of no practical interest to others.

The same atmosphere of confusion and doubt hangs over crop circle dowsing. Many dowsers are aware of this, and the best of them are also prone to doubts. They are nonetheless certain that the earth energy patterns which they detect at crop circle sites offer a most important clue to an overall understanding of the phenomenon.

Cerealogical dowsers include most of the leading crop circle researchers. The strictly scientific Dr. Meaden acknowledges from personal experience the efficacy of dowsing circles (see *The Crop Circle Enigma,* page 82) and attributes their charged energy field to the impact of an electrified plasma vortex, acting upon the chemicals in the soil (thus raising the interesting question of the possible role of field chemicals in the formation of circles). Another pioneer cerealogist, Richard Andrews, probably the most experienced dowser of them all, contributes an interesting chapter on crop circle dowsing to *The Crop Circle Enigma*. Also confirmed dowsers are the *Circular Evidence* authors, Pat Delgado and Colin Andrews, and so are Busty Taylor, Lucy Pringle, David Tilt, Hamish Miller and many others who are active in the cornfields. Bill Lewis, the veteran water diviner respected by all parties, has dowsed crop circles and describes them as fields of strongly activated energy which, he found, could be negated by metal objects placed at their nodal points.

It is thus impressively testified that crop circles are actively charged and have a peculiar energy field which any dowser can detect. Hardened sceptics may still dispute this, bringing up wishful thinking and the well-known receptivity of dowsers to the thoughts and ideas of others; and they are not entirely unreasonable in asking dowsers to conduct scientific tests among themselves. Yet the quality of the evidence from so many honest and well trained observers deserves at least further investigation.

These extracts from the writings of five notable dowsers are chosen with the idea of shedding light on questions which concern all cerealogists: What are the dowsers actually saying? Where do they agree and disagree? What picture is emerging from their combined insights into the nature of the crop circle phenomenon, and in what direction are their researches leading us?

Longwood Estate, June 1990—Richard Elen

SIG LONEGREN ON
THE BLIND MEN'S ELEPHANT

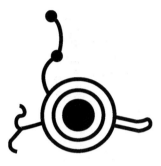

Cheesefoot Head—Richard Fraser

Author of Spiritual Dowsing *and a former Trustee of the American Society of Dowsers, Sig Lonegren of Vermont has been the most influential promoter of energy dowsing in America. For over twenty years he has investigated the astronomical, geometrical and earth energy characteristics of ancient stone chambers and monuments in the eastern United States in relation to sacred sites in Europe. His studies of crop circles began in 1989.*

There seem to be at least two quite different motivational factors that cause people to investigate sacred space. First, there are those who research these places to gain scientific knowledge. They utilise the scientific method where repeatability is a key criterion. If others cannot duplicate your findings, you have not complied with the rules of science, and therefore you cannot claim to have new knowledge. You do not have "truth". Dowsers who help archaeologists locate buried artifacts fall within this first category—either there are bones/pottery/ bronze daggers etc. where they say "dig" or there aren't.

A second group of people visit sacred sites looking for something quite different from what scientific researchers seek. These are pilgrims on the spiritual path, and they seek to utilise these sacred spaces for spiritual enlightenment. Those

Researcher Lucy Pringle picks up a strong pendulum reaction at a crop circle.

on the spiritual path do not necessarily employ scientific methodology, and it is not expected that their experience of the numinous will be consistent with others' experience. Between 1000BC and 1000AD there was a group of people— Buddha, Lao-tzu, Confucius, Zoroaster, Jesus and Mohammed among others—who experienced oneness with their Creator. Each experienced it differently. Over the last several millennia there have been various dogmatic religious sects that have demanded that there is only one correct way to see God. It just doesn't work that way. There are many different spiritual paths, and each one has its own vision of the One. Each spiritual path sees it differently, and it can not be proved that any particular path is the only correct one. Each aspirant must experience it for themselves and make up their own mind. It would be like asking a scientist to prove that there is a God: it can't be done.

Many who dowse for the energies at sacred sites fall within this second category. Each dowser sees it in their own way. (It is important for me to say at this point that I do not completely reject knowledge that has been collected through scientific methodology; however, it is definitely not the only tool I use to define "reality"—especially in the spiritual realms. In my writing, I encourage my readers to use both methods of gaining "truth"—both the intuitive and the rational. It is the wholistic way of approaching these mysteries.)

As a dowser with an abiding interest in sacred space, I have found the crop circles of the Wiltshire Downs to be a most exciting phenomenon. Before I tell what I have been finding, I need to say something about dowsing intangible targets. By 'intangible' I mean targets that can not be touched—like auras, thought forms and earth energies. Many dowsers are interested in tangible targets: places to drill for a well, where is the lost wedding ring, where is evidence of past civilisations. With tangible targets, empirical evidence is available. Either you hit the water, find the ring or the treasure or the ancient remains, or you don't; judgement is by results.

With intangible target dowsing, however, it isn't so easy. As a matter of fact, just the opposite of repeatability seems to be the case. It has been my experience over the last twenty years that no two dowsers at any given sacred space ever seem to find the same thing! I have put forth what I call 'Sig's hypothesis #1': "Unless they were trained by the same teacher, different dowsers will rarely find the same thing at a sacred site." There are many possible explanations why this is so. I feel we each bring our own level of consciousness to the dowsing experience, and also, we find what we expect to find. Swedish and German dowsers find grid lines, Fountain International dowsers find grape clusters and Maltese crosses, I find underground veins of primary water (yin) and energy leys (six- to eight-foot-wide beams of yang energy with a direction of flow) sometimes found running concurrently with leys—alignments of sacred sites.

Perhaps the best "reason" for all of these different dowsing results with intangible targets can be understood by using the analogy of the blind men and the elephant. Remember how they all found something different? As dowsers, as we're all basically new at this, we're all blind. While the field of Earth Energy dowsing is fifty years old, most people who see themselves as Earth Energy dowsers have been doing it for much less time than that—many for just a few years. We all "see" the Earth Energy elephant differently. In our present stage of development it's about as relevant for a scientist to put most dowsers to a scientific test and to expect that we'd find the same thing as it would be to apply Olympic equestrian judging standards to a nine-year old girl in her first year at riding school. We just won't live up to the scientific methodological requirement of repeatability. (I'm not convinced that it is even possible.)

John Michell is fond of saying that if you get twenty different artists to paint, say Silbury Hill, you will get twenty very different pictures of that ancient mound. The same seems to be true with intangible target dowsers. We all find something slightly different. Those who are researching these sites using only scientific methodology throw up their hands in disgust and draw the conclusion that dowsing is invalid. I, on the other hand, draw an entirely different conclusion. We each, as individuals, experience the spiritual realms in our own individual way—*vive la différence!*

Having said that, I would like to report what I have found. At each corn circle that I've visited, I found only underground veins of primary water. In the last two years, I've had the good fortune to visit crop circles in the Silbury Hill area, and the ones that appeared this year east of Warminster near the Devil's Punchbowl. I have yet to find an energy ley at one of these circles. This would then, according to this blind man's view of the elephant, not put these corn circles on what I would call power centres (a convergence of at least one vein of water and one energy ley). The sacred sites of Britain—Stonehenge, Avebury circle, Silbury Hill, West Kennet Long Barrow etc. are all on these power centres. Corn circles aren't.

Sig goes on to suggest that crop circles are messages from our prehistoric ancestors, warning us about the present state of the world. Through reincarnation, we are the same people as the ancients, so crop circles can be regarded as messages which we have sent to ourselves.

Newton St Loure, nr Bath, 1991—Richard Elen

Roland Pargeter

HAMISH MILLER ON THE
CONNECTION WITH ANCIENT SITES

East Kennet, 1991—Richard Fraser

An engineering graduate of St Andrews and Edinburgh Universities, Hamish Miller built up a large manufacturing company and then left it to become a blacksmith and metal sculptor in Cornwall. His recent book, The Sun and the Serpent, *written in partnership with Paul Broadhurst, tells the remarkable results of his dowsing investigations along the St Michael line (the apparent straight alignment of sanctuaries dedicated to the Archangel Michael which stretches between the extreme eastern and western points of England, with its centre at Avebury). Around this line he detected two oppositely charged streams of earth current, the 'Michael' and the 'Mary', which crossed each other at certain significant spots on the line. These findings have been confirmed by many other dowsers, including British Society of Dowsers officials. A number of crop circles, including some of the recent Avebury formations, have occurred on or very near these lines.*

In 1988 I happened upon the last huge Beckhampton circle just before it was harvested. Walking in through the tram lines led to an unforgettable moment when I reached the awesome, immaculate outer ring of the circle. It was my first close encounter and I could feel the hair rising on the back of my neck in recognition of the deep significance of the power behind this manifestation. It was much later, from the reports of the experts, that I realised just how important this circle was.

Paul Broadhurst

Hamish Miller dowsing a 1990 formation

Dowsing had to be fast if I was not to be flattened by a huge combine harvester, but I was able to establish a series of ten concentric rings of energy only inches apart, defining the outer perimeter of the main circle. Five similar bands spanned the outer ring and a number of radials—time prevented an accurate count—fanned out from the energy centre, a metre away from the swirl centre. Based on the configuration of the corn, my assumption, that the spiral vortex normally found at established earth energy centres would appear, turned out to be quite wrong, and in fact up till now, after dowsing upwards of fifty crop markings, I have not yet come across such a spiral.

There appeared to be no exit line until further probing led to the discovery that the complex connecting line not only had energy flowing in both directions but had components of 'male' and 'female' energy to boot. I use the terms male and female advisedly with the implication that there are a number of subtle differences between the energies which are not just positive and negative.

The forces involved have considerable range and it was easily possible to pick these lines up in an aircraft at 500 feet—doubly interesting for me as in one case the line had been dowsed on the ground heading over a hill and it was only at that height I could see the tumulus involved.

A stimulating new factor arose with the pictograms, on establishing that in the first one near Cheesefoot Head, the larger circle dowsed male while the smaller one was female, each having the now familiar ten-pointed star round its energy centre, but with considerable differences in the size of the outline. When the majestic Alton Barnes configuration appeared, the fascination was that while the larger circles were uniquely male or female the smaller ones registered both forms of energy—an androgynous form, or a beautifully balanced male/female manifestation?

Further dowsing showed that the configuration at the centre of the small circles was quite different and resembled a well squashed Teutonic cross. A similar contour was recorded in dowsed interpretations of earth energy fields in specific places some years ago, although in this case the contour was much nearer to the recognised Teutonic cross proportion.

There was no discernible deterioration in the strength and shape of the energy field after the crop had been cut, and little apparent difference some weeks later after ploughing, although in truth it is extremely difficult to be specific without a positive datum to work from.

The hoaxes, of course, have no such energy fields and any dowser with a little experience will establish the authenticity of a crop circle in pretty quick time. Interesting though, in the case of the notorious KLF logo circle, it was possible to wind up through a number of levels of dowsing to find a faint ghostly response to the "intent" of the people who spent so much time making it.

There is an indefinable lament to the art of dowsing which at this stage almost precludes the establishment of absolute date, particularly for those whose narrow disciplines require results written in concrete before they are acceptable. I believe that it is important to submit all data as it is honestly found, rather than selected items geared to shore up a pet theory.

Dowsing is not yet an exact science, since most people work on a fairly wide band of frequencies. Even practised operatives, specialising in the same field, work in marginally different wavelengths and the results can sometimes be difficult to reconcile. However if each dowser presents data truthfully and is acutely aware of the ever-present danger of indulging the required results, some consistent meaningful stuff will emerge. This should be made available to all other disciplines to consider, accept or reject freely.

Perhaps the most shattering discovery made during this brief time was in finding at the centre a sixteen-foot twelve-pointed star configuration, quite remarkably similar to the contour which we had been dowsing at sites on the Michael Line where the male and female energies crossed each other at particularly sacred places.

A hasty exit to avoid being baled precluded any further work, and it was not until late May '90, through John Haddington's Crop Watch, that a further opportunity arose to dowse many of the exciting new formations, including the pictograms around Cheesefoot Head.

Earlier in the year—over Beltane in fact—I had been working at Avebury and discovered that the 12-pointed star configuration at the energy crossing points on the line had developed through an amorphous nine-petal shape to move into the next stage as a ten-pointed star. These evolving configurations have been recorded over the last few years by a number of independent dowsers all over the country and abroad, but since at the moment there is no physical manifestation of the force fields, their accurate definition is a little difficult. Mind you, I realised with a heart-stopping sense of wonder that the configuration within the circle had followed the changing pattern of the earth energy and was now in tune with the most important ancient sites in the area.

The disciplines of not inducing the results one wants to find are quite fierce, and a considerable effort has to be made to make sure that the dowsing interpretations are honest.

I found at first some problems in concentrating long enough to do an accurate count of the radials from the centre, and on a number of occasions during the process I forgot where I put the start marker, or forgot what I had used as a marker, lost the simple count, or was distracted by some triviality.

Three times, after lots of practice in maintaining the concentration needed, I experienced what I can only describe as a time slip. The radials count would go 5-6-7-10 and I would find myself at a considerably different part of the circle on the count of ten from where I had been on the count of seven. I believe that this effect has been felt in various ways by other observers, where problems in concentration have affected those dealing with photography and measurement. Perhaps the force fields within the circles have an influence on our own biomagnetic fields.

In all the cases I managed to dowse, the number of lines of energy defining the shape of the formation seemed to be in multiples of five: *i.e.*, 10 concentric rings powerfully defining the outer rim of the circles with the bands sometimes only half an inch apart; wide straight avenues with ten or twenty bands; narrow features including in certain pictograms, the 'littlehands' or 'spanner' with fine bands and a quite remarkable consistency of twenty radials from the energy centres.

Perhaps it's worth noting that all the stone circles and standing stones in the West Penwith area of Cornwall, with one or two very specific exceptions, have 20 radials of energy coming from their centre, but they have an additional spiral vortex which pulses particularly with moon cycles and also quite dramatically in response to our growing recognition that it's there.

The logistics of the astonishing tuning-in of the force fields within the circles to the ancient landscape were reinforced when I became aware that one of the first pictograms had a strong energy line connection with a local tumulus. Checks showed that all the crop markings that I dowsed later had such a connection, though not necessarily with the closest tumulus. The Beckhampton 'Comma' line passed within a whisker of the triangle on its way to the large tumulus to the west, while the triangle hooked into the long barrow in the field below the Longstones.

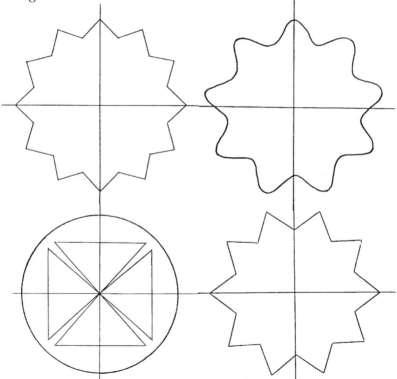

Patterns of earth energy fields dowsed at crop formations by Hamish Miller. 12-, 9- and 10-pointed figures are shown and a Teutonic cross. The latter was dowsed at the centre of the smaller circles at Alton Barnes in 1990.

It is inevitable while researching these ancient and modern energy phenomena that one becomes open to further peripheral experiences in association with the main work. About fifteen months into the Michael Line, and subsequently on crop circles, I became aware of the feeling of being observed. I am a practical, well earthed being, earning my living as a blacksmith, but I had to concede after some time that the number of the 'Watchers', as they came to be called, seemed to increase. Later we even appeared to hear a slight susurrus of discussion round us, and have a deeply entrenched impression of beings of a vastly different culture strolling languidly but interestedly around chatting about what we were doing.

I had a chance to discuss this with Alex Neklessa, the Russian scientist who has his own Institute for Paranormal Studies near Moscow. Alex works with an extraordinary team of scientists and mystics and one of his projects was to experiment with strictly-controlled regression to previous civilisations in order to find out what went wrong with them. An astonishing result seemed to indicate a probability that, in certain cases, two or three parallel realities existed at the same time.

If this was the case, and it appears to be rather more than idle conjecture, is it possible that in our time such a situation could obtain? And, if so, could a group of highly intelligent and technically advanced beings, living in parallel with us, but in a slightly different time scale, be a little concerned about how we in our wisdom are treating our planetary parent body? And are we receiving a gentle nudge to make us aware that we are not alone, and that we have responsibilities to a wider concept of beings than we have been aware of up till now?

I put it forward as a matter for quiet consideration, since it may provide stimulus for the re-assessment of many legends, cults, religions and belief systems.

My own feelings during a most privileged involvement in these mysteries are that at all times, including deep meditation at stone and crop circles, there is a totally benign intelligent guiding power with a huge compassion behind these manifestations. The only time I have had such a profound experience was in an out-of-body journey after an emergency in 1982.

I confess I am looking forward with some impatience to see what sophisticated artistry will appear next year.

Alton Barnes, 1990—Richard Elen

DAVID TILT ON CROP CIRCLES AND AN ANCIENT ENERGY SYSTEM

'Insectogram' near Stonehenge, 1991—Richard Elen

Since 1983 David Tilt of Sussex has been tracing the paths and centres of an energy system which, he believes, was laid out across the landscape by an ancient priesthood. He has published details of it, and about its connection to UFOs, crop circles and other strange phenomena, in the Journal of the British Society of Dowsers and elsewhere. Here he explains the formation of crop circles through energy discharges from this system, conducted by crystals in the soil.

In the summer of 1983 I commenced a project of dowsing prehistoric sites, and the lines of energy that link them. The project was prompted by my discovery of a henge site where many lines of energy appear to have been tapped in a numerical sequence which relates to fifty-six pits on the perimeter of the sites—similar to Stonehenge. This was the first indication that an unusual skill, hitherto only suspected, had been practised in prehistory. It also provided the basis for tracing many lines of energy across the countryside to other sites, and landscape features associated with a vast circuit of energy. As the project developed it became apparent that the network of energy is also linked to a broad spectrum of paranormal phenomena, including the phenomenon of crop circles and the enigma of some UFO sightings, particularly the strange lights often seen in close proximity to prehistoric sites. The link between the circles and the UFO phenomenon should be by now beyond reasonable doubt.

As far as I know, no one has yet determined the precise method used to tap or draw off energy, and to run lines of energy across the landscape. The little archaeological evidence available suggests it may have been done by using shaped slivers of flint. Whatever the method, there appears to be some extraordinary knowledge behind it, because the main source of the energy appears to be naturally sited quartz. A piece of quartz radiates the same outward flowing 'type A' energy pattern as that dowsed at the henge, where its orientation suggests a magnetic polar factor.

In a practical sense, the creation of the energy system appears to have been achieved by constructing most of the prehistoric sites in relation to underground water, and linking them with lines of energy. This is significant because a column of underground water has its own electrical field which can be located by dowsing. Electricity, magnetism, and water appear to be fundamental to the system. The henge discovered in 1983 is situated on a geological boundary, and is also in an area where there is quartz from Pliocene drift deposits. This implies that the source of the energy there is probably quartz trapped under pressure between two geological surfaces. A short distance away from the henge there is another similar, but smaller, energy pattern further along the geological boundary; this pattern is untapped and in its natural state. Trapped quartz could be one of the reasons, the other being water, why the energy level of the system reaches a peak five to six days after new moon, and goes slightly lower close to full moon. Lunar gravitational effects on water and the land mass are well-known. Furthermore, the piezo-electric properties of quartz cause it to build up a substantial electrical charge when it is subjected to pressure. It also oscillates, so I was not surprised to discover, by using a diode receiver (the modern version of a crystal set), coupled to a tape recorder, that very strong pulsating signals can be detected and

Tom Fenn

David Tilt uses a diode receiver and portable tape recorder to capture radio signal emissions from a circle near Lewes, Sussex, in 1990

recorded at the henge, and also at some of the mounds elsewhere in the countryside, particularly those with radiating energy lines from their centres. These mounds, like some of the tumuli, are similar to electrical distribution points because they have a supply line coming in from a henge and multiple lines of energy flowing out.

Crop circles are not caused by whirlwinds, tornadoes, or any meteorological phenomenon, neither are they the result of UFOs landing. The answer appears to lie with the 'type A' energy pattern found at the henges, and its apparent period energy discharges. At certain times, the energy charge becomes so great it overflows and discharges itself. When this happens, air which is normally non-conducting becomes a conductor in the vicinity of the strong electrical field and carries the charge away from a number of places on the 'type A' energy pattern. This causes what is known as an 'electric wind' which can make crop circles at henge sites, if they are covered by a tall crop. When a discharge occurs the energy also overflows along the main energy lines from the site. This can cause a circle to appear away from the site, at energy line junction points, and at places where tumuli have been removed (tumuli are like electrical distribution points). It is highly probable that the more complex circles where the crop is flattened in clockwise and counter-clockwise directions, are caused by almost simultaneous energy discharges at different locations, and the resulting conflicting energy flows. What I found so interesting is the apparent intelligent use of the energy in the formation of some crop circles.

In July 1989, I examined a crop circle at Cheesefoot Head, Hampshire. This circle had appeared where a tumulus has been removed—eleven lines of energy radiate from an area approximately 2 metres in diameter at the centre of the circle. This is similar to the tumuli I have examined in Sussex, and is further confirmation that the energy system is definitely involved in the creation of crop circles.

Tom Fenn

David Tilt with dowsing rods demonstrates energy transmission from eight points from the circle in the middle of a formation at Lewes, Sussex, 1990.

A first indication of this occurred in 1984. During the night of 27/28th July, a set of five crop circles in the shape of a cross appeared in a field of wheat at Rathfinny Farm near Seaford, Sussex. I had been working on a henge site further inland until the afternoon of the 28th. The 'energy level at this site had increased to an unbearable degree making it extremely unpleasant to continue dowsing there. Under these conditions disorientation, dizziness, and difficulty in concentration are experienced, and this type of site is best left alone until the energy decreases to a more tolerable level. When I returned there on the 3rd of August, I was certain something unusual had happened because the energy level was exceptionally low. At the back of my mind was the similarity between the crossed alignment of the circles that had appeared at Rathfinny—with

Lewes, Sussex, 1990 (see photographs on pages 27 & 29)—Roland Pargeter

the largest circle at the centre—and the 'type A' energy pattern at the henge site. There were no visible signs at the henge because the site was covered by short grass. However, about 350 yards away on one of the main energy lines from the site, there is a T junction energy line tapping point where another line has been run off in a different direction. This point is in an isolated spot which at the time was overgrown with long grass. The T junction can be dowsed as a square pit about a metre across. In dry conditions with little grass it is visible as a square indentation in the ground. I subsequently discovered that the grass surrounding this tapping point had been flattened in a clockwise spiral creating a perfect circle some 2 metres in diameter. Another clockwise circle, 3.35 metres in diameter, appeared in wheat at the same place in July 1990.

In late June 1990, I carried out a detailed examination of a dumb-bell shaped crop circle configuration at Cheesefoot Head. This had appeared on an energy line which flows from the direction of the Longwood Estate. Prior to my arrival, another dowser, Richard Andrews, had also made a detailed examination of this configuration. Richard specialises in dowsing a layer or level of energy above the ground while I have always been primarily concerned with the archaeological layout of energy lines *in* the ground. When we compared our respective plans of this configuration they were remarkably similar, except for one interesting fact—the energy line flow in the upper level was the reverse of that in the ground. The circle nearest the Longwood Estate had fifteen energy lines radiating from an area about 2 metres in diameter at the centre of the circle. This is similar to the energy lines at tumuli. Four of these radiating energy lines led to rectangular impressions in the crop where there were dowsing indications of vortices. These were also noticeable in a narrow band around the perimeter of the circle where the crop had been flattened in an alternate direction. The trough connecting the two circles—hence the dumb-bell shape—had appeared along the energy line from the Longwood Estate; this also passed through the remaining circle which had twenty energy lines radiating from a 2 metre area at its centre.

Since returning to Sussex, I have carried out a number of tests at tumuli, along energy lines, and also at the henge site mentioned above. The energy from an energy line fans out in a upward flow to approximately 1 metre above the ground where it connects with another layer or level of energy. Continuing its upward flow above this level, the energy fans inwards until it reaches a further layer or level of energy about 2 metres above the ground. In other words, the flow from the ground to the third level assumes a diamond shape. This appears to be particularly significant in relation to the constant use of diamond shapes, some of which are believed to be shadow pits, at prehistoric sites. The energy flow in each level is alternate. Recordings taken by using a Sony *TCM-3* cassette recorder, connected to a diode receiver fitted with a 2.5 mH RF choke, revealed a difference between the signal pulses detected in the archaeological energy ley-line level in the ground, and in each of the two levels above the ground. Level 3 is the most interesting having significantly faster signal pulses.

Crawley, north of Salisbury, 1990—Richard Elen

RICHARD ANDREWS ON ENERGY
PATTERNS BEHIND CIRCLE FORMATIONS

In his contribution to The Crop Circle Enigma, *Richard Andrews describes the methods of dowsing crop circles which he has developed from the early days of the phenomenon. He is an agricultural expert, a former Wessex farmer and a lifelong observer of nature's subtleties. A natural dowser, his awareness of vital energy lines in the earth (which he calls, to the distress of Watkins's followers, 'ley lines') was sharpened by investigations at ancient sites, and he emphasises the energy connection between prehistoric monuments and crop circles. His perception is that crop formations occur at spots where the patterns of earth energy have created a 'blueprint' which is later 'fired' to produce visible circle effects. Thus the sites and forms of crop circles are predetermined by the earth and can be predicted by alert dowsers. The modern occurrence of crop circles is linked to the dramatically intensified strength of earth energy currents over recent years, as observed by dowsers.*

I have studied the Corn Circle Phenomenon since 1985, when life in this subject was relatively uncomplicated. At this time I realised that the dowsing I had been doing for the past fifteen years on ley lines, or the energy grid associated with ancient megalithic sites, was also part of the Corn Circle Phenomenon.

To start with, there were single circles in varying sizes and groups of two and three. In 1983, the Quintuplet (that is, a large

Richard Andrews demonstrating dowsing with angle-rods to a TV crew from Australia's Channel 9.

circle with four satellites) first appeared at Cheesefoot Head, near Winchester. In 1986 the first single-ringed circle appeared. In 1988 a two-ringed circle and also three circles grouped together like a triangle. The last configuration of 1988 was a quintuplet with a ring round the satellites, as seen on the cover of *Circular Evidence*. The other significant happening in 1988 was that the quintuplets on some sites doubled in size, and the number of circles reached approximately 100. This was a quantum leap in the Corn Circle Phenomenon.

1989 saw the number of circles double again with all the previous circle configurations in evidence, but the final two circles of the season, at Winterbourne Stoke, were of a new type which has not so far been repeated. The second configuration was a quartered circle, its photograph by Busty Taylor being the front cover of *The Corn Circle Enigma*.

1990 showed a complete departure from the traditional configurations, producing large pictograms, *i.e.*, circles, triangles, wings, finger and key patterns. The dowsable patterns have also changed very substantially with the widening and amalgamation of lines, which is a new feature evolving in conjunction with the new patterns.

Many people are now showing interest in the subject, and it is very gratifying that my original work on dowsing has now become standard practice for verifying circles. I have proved beyond doubt that all genuine circle configurations have a dowsable print, and that the hoax will not leave any relevant print. Although there is no need to fear these sudden manifestations, there is need for caution, however, because the energies present can be very powerful indeed and some people will be affected physically by experiencing headaches and nausea, while others will experience depression or great elation. When any of these symptoms occur, the best antidote is to retreat from the circle configuration immediately and the symptoms will recede within an hour or so. Others, however, will experience none of these effects.

I hope this will begin to show that there is very much more here than we would have appreciated a few years ago, and that quick answers to this wonderful happening are too early. We are only part way through a very complex weave of experience and reality, which will need some of the best minds brought to bear to begin to show the right pathways to tread.

Dowsing is a tool that has created a window for us to look through and begin to see some of these pathways. I believe this to be the Renaissance for the human experience. Let us go quietly and steadily forward and bring stability out of chaos, and understand our part in the ecological and metaphysical maze shown in this phenomenon.

Dowsing with angle rods

The three-line ley is the main reference for the circle configuration, as the circles themselves are positioned centrally between these lines. All circle configurations have crossing positive lines in the centre which will produce the positive response in the dowsing rods (crossing each other inwards, while one rod held away from the body over the centre of the circle, or node point, will rotate). One of these lines will be parallel to the three-line leys while the other will be at approximately 90° to them. Circles in the main have 5, 7 or 9 dowsable rings. Starting from the centre of the circle, the first ring will move both dowsing rods to the left, the second to the right, the third to the left and so on, always ending the circle itself with both rods pointing outwards, away from each other, *i.e.* a negative response. This is the practice for locating the circle print at any time of the year.

In the summer, when the circle has appeared in the corn, the marking of the three-line leys and the centre positive line with pegs on the headland of the field will give easy reference out of season. Always photograph floor patterns before entering any circle.

Some circles will have two centres approximately half a metre apart. The reason for this is that the width of the lines have increased and the nodes will be on either side of that line, where the other line crosses in the centre of the circle. For measuring the circle, you will have to decide from which centre you will take your measurements, and ensure that this is the one used for *all* measurements. First take the compass bearings and then measure the radius to the four compass points. On arriving at the fourth measurement, leave the tape stretched from the centre to the edge and now take the two dowsing rods, checking the centre first and then walking along the tape to note the number and position of the rings. After this has been done, check to see if there are any other responses on your rods and endeavour to identify the meaning of the response. When the circle configuration is a quintuplet the four satellites will be positioned on the crossing lines.

Expanding lines

1989 was particularly productive from the dowsing point of view. I discovered that on either side and on the edge of certain three-line leys a wavy line had appeared. Over the course of ten days they expanded until in one case they embraced a small circle configuration on either side. The same occurred at a similar site, some six metres away, which is near an example of what I call a Master Print—a dowsed multiple pattern of which only part will show as a circle in the corn.

As these circles grew in size over three weeks, I thought that when the two circles touched each other I would have found the trigger to a circle in the corn. But this was not so. Instead of touching, the easterly three-line ley started to move away from the westerly one, and then a single line came between the two circles. Then they began to show a second circle within the small one. As the single line moved from left to right, so the two circles grew and diminished correspondingly. Then, on a daily basis, the circle configurations changed and after three months were beginning to show similar floor patterns to those found at Winterbourne Stoke.

Even more interesting, the three-line leys were more than twenty metres apart, and the dowsable circle between them was the same diameter as the fired circles in the field. I call this a Seeding Pattern, as I found out later that the circles were travelling between the vertical three-line leys and stopping on horizontals. A similar area was dowsed some four miles away, on what turned out to be the same two lines, about 8 hours different in timing. Over the year, there was a sequence of three similar formations. As yet these have not shown physically, but who knows what may happen in the future!

Pictograms 1990

The first of the pictograms, a dumbbell configuration, appeared on May 23rd/24th at Chilcomb near Winchester. From the dowsing point of view, this appeared to be the greatest challenge yet to the work I had been doing. I was relieved to find that it had a full dowsable pattern of quite unusual nature. The two circles at either end of the shaft dowsed as expected. The shaft that joined them was the same width as the line that went through the middle of both circles, but the second half of that shaft diminished to half size. This was consistent with the work done on the expanding lines in the centre of circles, when I found the reason they were getting wider was because they were an amalgamation of lines, and on this particular line both the wider and the accompanying line had shown up separately.

The next puzzle was the four boxes—two either side of the shaft. Why did we have rectangular shapes of similar size equidistant from the shaft, and starting and terminating where they did? This was revealed when I found they were as long as the width of a three-line ley which ran horizontally through the shaft.

The next problem was, why were there four? On dowsing the larger circle pattern, I found there were five vertical lines, one of which was the central shaft between two circles, and the other four lines were the same width as the boxes. The most fascinating observation in the boxes was that the lie of the corn was reversed on the edges nearest the centre shaft, and the rest of the boxes were lying in the same direction as the shaft.

Later, when I was dowsing the third pictogram, I found that one side of the three-line ley was positive and the other side negative. It appeared that the current fired from one and bounced back from the other and earthed as would an electrical current, leaving a clear combed effect at the top of the

Chilcomb, 1990 (see text)—Richard Elen

boxes. This is the first time this particular combing had appeared.

If there is no three-line ley going through the shaft of a pictogram there will not be any boxes. If there are five lines parallel vertically, there will be four boxes; if there are three lines parallel vertically, there will be four boxes; while three lines parallel will produce two boxes.

The dowsable pattern within pictograms is now very complex, and I have found there to be seven different levels in some of them, apart from other side effects, and the use of diagonal lines by the pictograms. This is just the beginning of a greater understanding and a glimpse of what may be revealed in the coming years.

Etchilhampton, 1990, spoke added—Richard Elen

Roland Pargeter

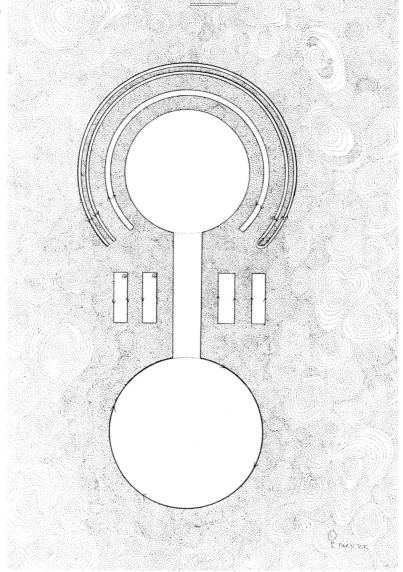

COLIN BLOY'S AXIOMS AND EXPERIENCES

Bath, Avon—Richard Fraser

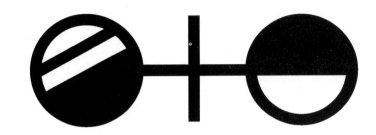

The founder of Fountain International (for restoring harmony within and between humanity and the living earth through psychic and spiritual means), Colin Bloy is a man of many parts: politician, businessman, dowser, spiritual revivalist and much else. He lives in Brighton.

Dowsing is not a uniquely physiological phenomenon. Dowsing apparatus, be they rods, pendulums or hands, indicate a self-induced reaction; they are a form of link between the rational mind and the consciousness. Here are some axioms.

• **You cannot find by dowsing what you are not looking for.**
• **You cannot find what you cannot conceive of.**
• **You can find what you want and can conceive of, so long as you maintain clarity and alertness and visualise what you are looking for.** Whereas dowsers may agree on conclusions, they don't all use the same means of recognition.

Thus what follows is idiosyncratic, and by no test can it be guaranteed as complete so far as circle energies are concerned, partly because of the problem of formulating the correct concepts in a novel area.

In metaphysical and physical terms, my premise is that all reality is in the same continuum, and that energies in the ley system are subtle, universal and an aspect of consciousness.

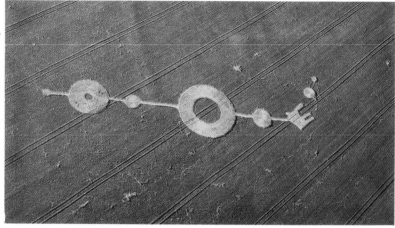

Preshute Down, 1991—Roland Pargeter

Thus the hypothesis that circles would impact upon the system was the first to come to mind.

While the crops are standing, it is very difficult to dowse outside and around a circle, but I soon became aware that energy lines from circles connected in to established node-points within the system, which thus encouraged further studies within the circles themselves.

Thus, when entering those double-linked circles, first at Cheesefoot Head, my object was to see what related energies were inside the circles.

For various reasons, primarily involving what one might call 'Fountain' activity, a very fine grid pattern exists in many countries of the world. Each square in the grid has a side of 8mm.

Events such as air crashes and other violent occurrences tear a large hole many hundreds of yards in diameter around the epicentre.

Approaching a dumb-bell formation at Cheesefoot Head, it was apparent that the event had caused a similar hole, about 100 yards in radius, and this phenomenon appears constant in respect of other circles.

The next observation, and keeping the mind on 'ley', or subtle energies, was that the outline or silhouette of circle formations is equally dowsable.

Within the double circles, there was a clear dowsable distinction between the two, which once again is common to others.

In one, I found a 16-loop spiral within a dowsable circle.

In the other circle, instead of a spiral there were 16 concentric circles. Sensitives with me at the time felt more relaxed in the concentric circles.

In other circles the number of loops in the spirals was 8, as also in the concentric circles. I should add that they do change, and can go to 64 and more, but always a multiple of 8.

Dowsing, leaning over the circles, but without damaging the crops, it was possible to notice putative radials, which would seem to confirm Hamish Miller's point. The number varied, but seemed to be based on an 8 factor.

And when Michael Omejer played his harp in the relatively unknown pictogram under Milk Hill, which was just as big as Alton Barnes, the circles and the spirals expanded greatly, as did parallel lines in the central avenue of the figure.

I have issued caveats about the nature of dowsing, and there may well have been energies of which I was not able to conceive. However my conclusion, based on my own personal experience, is that there is nothing in the circles that I visited which gave cause for anything other than joy. That they should manifest the twin essential energies of healing, dragon and cosmos, is all to the good.

I can quite understand that certain people would feel wobbly in a circle, if they do not adjust to the energy, but I would be very surprised if anyone were seriously affected negatively for any period of time.

Now it is difficult to dowse around a pictogram before the harvest, for fear of damaging the corn. Richard Andrews and I agreed that, at Alton Barnes, there was an energy line from the pictogram going in the general direction of the tumulus called Adam's Grave. On another occasion, I saw fit to dowse the local churches and found that the "conventional" energies were greater by a factor of ten or more—not the church of Alton Barnes, incidentally, but the church of Alton Priory. After, I asked Mrs David Carson about that, and she said that the field in question was in the parish of Alton Priory, not Alton Barnes, but the farmhouse was in Alton Barnes, hence the misattribution.

Later on, when the circle epidemic struck Sussex, and particularly Brighton, I was able to confirm that the new configurations had the same effect on the local parish church. All energy patterns were based on an 8 factor.

Barbury Castle, 1991—Richard Elen

Assessment
by John Michell

Telegraph Hill, Chilcomb, 1990—Richard Elen

The dowsers we have heard from are generally agreed—Sig Lonegren being the one exception—that all genuine crop circles conform to organised energy fields in the earth. These energy patterns are the same as those which the dowsers find at ancient mounds, tumuli and stone circles. Tilt, Miller, Andrews, Bloy and other dowsers say that crop circles are joined by strong, straight lines of energy to nearby tumuli.

When it comes to the details of the patterns they discern at crop circles, the dowsers are widely at variance with each other. Mostly they report concentric energy rings around the centre, and some of them describe radial spokes as well, but the diagrams they produce of these features are quite strikingly different. Each dowser seems to have his favourite number. Miller finds rings in numbers of 5 or 10, Bloy sees everything in 8s and 16s, Andrews says that circles have 5, 7 or 9 dowsable rings, while Tilt has a more sophisticated number system based on 56. Such diversity among so few seems almost beyond chance!

Confronted with their discrepancies, dowsers have recourse to Sig's elephant and admit that they are each attuned to a mere part of the whole. This is well expressed by Pat Delgado in the very suggestive last chapter of *The Latest Evidence*. Having tried rods and pendulums, he gave them both up, with the following results.

"I soon realised rods were a hindrance to progress in understanding more about the energies surrounding us. During a session dowsing a tumulus, I became aware I was detecting only a tiny fraction of what was there to be discovered. I abandoned the rods and started to use my bare hands. Immediately a whole new world of information opened up. It was the beginning of my really understanding energies and the intelligence that controls them."

Pat's understanding is similar to Richard Andrews', that the creation of crop circles proceeds in two stages. First, an intelligent force from above draws an invisible plan over a field, working as if with rapid strokes of a brush to predetermine the direction in which every cornstalk will fall. At the second stage, some time after, a force from below the ground 'fires' the pattern and makes it visible as a crop formation. Both the designing and the actualising of every crop circle are determined by an unknown will and executed by unknown agents.

The dowsers have all warned us that we must expect inconsistencies between their various statements because each of them is attuned to a different level of the overall energy field. David Tilt speaks literally of these levels when he compares his ground level with Richard Andrews' above-ground dowsing. This is surely acceptable, and we can be grateful for the dowsers for reporting honestly their individual results without recourse to conspiracies. Their frankness about their differences makes it all the more impressive when they speak with one voice. Dowsers are notoriously individual, holding fast to their own views, methods and means to insight, but on the subject of crop circles, despite many stylistic differences (similar to the differences which arise when a group of artists draw from the same model), there is wide agreement among them. None of them may entirely agree with the summary below, but it is distilled from their statements and nearly represents the gist of what they are saying.

John Michell

According to what the dowsers are telling us, modern studies of the peculiar energy fields which they find at ancient sites have been followed in the last few years by the strengthening of those energies. Ancient links between the sites have been reanimated, restoring a prehistoric network of spiritual power. In traditional terms, the earth's subtle body, its *ch'i*, as recognised by acupuncturists in the human body, has somehow been stimulated and is now powerfully charged. The charge has spilled over from the ancient centres, leaping to nearby spots to produce corn circles. This process is not automatic or random but is directed by an unknown mind.

Symbols are appearing which no one understands, not even the dowsers. We are being directed to remember something, or

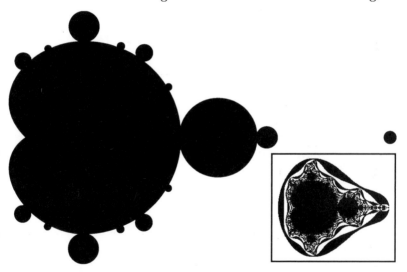

Cambridgeshire 'Mandelbrot', 1991—Richard Fraser

One of the last and most spectacular formations of 1991, this pattern appeared briefly in a field in Cambridgeshire. It is a well-known mathematical configuration known as a 'fractal' in which the basic figure is the same no matter how much it is magnified. This specific kind of fractal is often referred to as the 'Mandelbrot Set' after Benoît Mandelbrot who did much of the original work on fractal mathematics. Based on an aerial photograph, the above illustration was overlaid on a computer-generated version of the same fractal (inset): the two matched perfectly, even allowing for transcription errors. The position of the outlying circle is also mathematically accurate.

to search our own consciences for meanings which are being conveyed and which, no doubt, we already know. There are no fixed instructions, no code to be cracked, but a very precise message is being sent, directly into our minds. Such is the nature of those traditional portents which are apparent in periods of radical changes, when the archetypes are renewed, human minds are purged of illusions built up during the previous era, common sense reasserts itself and the normal, human, spiritual perception of reality is regained.

From the sublime to the practical: since dowsers claim that they can readily tell a genuine from a man-made circle, and since that ability will be very useful in future years when numerous hoaxes may be expected, perhaps crop circle dowsers should devise tests for themselves so that everyone would know the extent to which they can be relied on. In everyday dowsing, for water or minerals, their abilities are constantly tested by their need for successful results. There is no reason, therefore, why energy dowsers should be inhibited in letting us know who among them is best qualified to tell a real circle from a false one.